OUT AND ABOUT

OUT AND ABOUT

Preparing Children with Autism Spectrum Disorders to Participate in Their Communities

Jill Hudson

Amy Bixler Coffin

APC
P.O. Box 23173
Shawnee Mission, Kansas 66283-0173
www.asperger.net

© 2007 Autism Asperger Publishing Co.
P.O. Box 23173
Shawnee Mission, Kansas 66283-0173
www.asperger.net

Publisher's Cataloging-in-Publication

Hudson, Jill.
    Out and about : preparing children with autism spectrum disorders to participate in their communities / Jill Hudson, Amy Bixler Coffin. --
1st ed. -- Shawnee Mission, Kan. : Autism Asperger Pub. Co., 2007.
        p. ; cm.

        ISBN-13: 978-1-931282-48-2
        ISBN-10: 1-931282-48-X
        LCCN: 2007927745
        Includes bibliographical references (p. 77).

        1. Autistic children--Recreation. 2. Autism in children.
3. Community life. 4. Social participation. I. Coffin, Amy Bixler.
II. Title.

RJ506.A9 H83 2007
618.92/85882--dc22 0706

This book is designed in Jigsaw, Gill Sans and Zalderdash.

Printed in the United States of America.

TABLE OF CONTENTS

INTRODUCTION

Trey, a 6-year-old diagnosed with Asperger Syndrome, joined his first-grade class for the end-of-the-year picnic at the park. Trey loves the movie Finding Nemo *and now has a special interest of looking for fish. He loves to search for fish whenever he is around water; not surprisingly, the pond at the park was his perfect next target. Instead of staying with his peers in the pavilion and eating his lunch, he immediately ventured off to the pond. Delighted to see a real fish, Trey got so excited that he fell into the shallow pond as he tried to catch the fast-moving goldfish. While this posed no immediate danger to his safety, he nevertheless had to ride back on the bus in soaking-wet clothes and was frustrated that the fish got away.*

Children with autism spectrum disorders (ASD) are a vital part of their communities due to the special talents and unique interests that they can contribute. They have the ability and usually the desire to participate; however, often they go unnoticed, or are undervalued, and opportunities to interact with the world around them pass them by. Typically, the public in general is unaware of and unable to appreciate these unique characteristics, talents, and interests because of their lack of fully understanding autism spectrum disorders. Parents and educators are also sometimes hesitant or reluctant to permit children with ASD to fully participate in community activities because of a lack of supports.

By reviewing the details of an upcoming event or trip and building in support ahead of time, children with ASD will be successful as they interact with their communities, and adults will be more confident in letting them participate and bringing them along, if even just to the grocery store.

Autism spectrum disorders cover a range of abilities and challenges. Depending on when and which characteristics children present, they may receive a specific diagnosis as having either autism, Asperger Syndrome, or pervasive developmental disorder-not otherwise specified (PDD-NOS). Common core characteristics include social deficits, a delay in communication, varying levels of cognitive functions, impaired motor skills, repetitive behaviors, emotional vulnerability, and sensory sensitivities. These characteristics are unique in the manner in which they present in each child (Bregman, Zager, & Gerdtz, 2005; Myles & Adreon, 2001; Olley, 2005).

Community events are unique in the manner in which they will affect the individual at a given time due to the responses required and the ASD characteristic involved. That is, events vary ...

- in the degree to which the child is engaged – from simple participation to observation, to active involvement;

- in the amount of sensory stimuli generated, such as bowling pins crashing down versus the quiet environment in the library;

- in the number of people present; and

- in the level of familiarity of the venue for the child – a first-time event versus a place the child goes to routinely.

For these reasons, and because of the unique characteristics of persons with ASD, individual consideration must be given to the child and the particular community event as supports are determined and implemented. When a child has access to supports, meaning that strategies or interventions that address his needs are readily available and have been planned in advance, the chances of a successful event are significantly increased.

To illustrate, let's return to Trey from the opening vignette and see how advance planning could have made for a much more successful outing for everybody involved.

Before going to the park for the end-of-the-year class picnic, Mrs. Robinson, Trey's teacher, created a Blueprint. Because she knew that Trey's favorite movie was Finding Nemo, she created a Power Card using Nemo as the character of interest. She also incorporated the use of First eat lunch … Then look at fish together with an adult. Realizing that Trey enjoys water and gets excited when he sees a fish, she made a visual for him to stand on, providing him with a visual cue of how close he was allowed to be to the water. After finding fish in the pond, Trey was delighted to draw a picture of each fish he found and make a mural with them when he returned to his classroom at school. With these supports, Trey had fun on his class trip and was better able to follow the rules.

ABOUT THIS BOOK

The purpose of this book is to provide a framework for identifying the areas where an individual with ASD may need support to participate more fully and successfully in community outings.

The framework, created as a Blueprint, lists 10 tools identified in best practice as effective types of support for children with ASD. They range in nature from broad to more specific. The Blueprint can be used with children all across the spectrum, at all age and developmental levels, and for any community outing.

Because children with ASD will interact with the community under the leadership of a variety of adults, such as family members, educators, service providers, or other community members, the Blueprint has been created so that anyone may complete it by filling in the tools with the support that best matches the child for the event. For example, the Scout leader completes it so that the child with ASD is able to join his troop on a campout, the school teacher fills in the Blueprint to enable the child to successfully attend the fourth-grade field trip, and the family refers to it to ensure a successful and fun dinner out.

The community provides a vast array of opportunities for children to participate in, including sporting events, going to a birthday party at the skating rink, or strolling through the zoo. Throughout the book, examples are grouped within categories of places and situations that children are likely to encounter. The situations included are in no way all-inclusive, but consist of a broad range of examples from the categories of recreational activities, restaurants, stores, appointments, public services, taking trips, and special events.

The hope is that the specially designed Blueprint will become second nature to its users as they become more familiar with the areas of support the child needs in various situations and routinely use the Blueprint for different outings and different children. Eventually, the Blueprint may be completed mentally, implemented across multiple settings, and even adapted for a spontaneous trip when there is not much forewarning or time to plan, such as having to quickly run an errand to the grocery store on the way home from soccer practice, adapt the school schedule to include an impromptu student recognition assembly, or make an emergency trip to the hospital.

THE BLUEPRINT

The Blueprint outlines 10 tools to consider when identifying supports for a child with ASD in relation to a particular outing, including:

- Waiting plan
- Communication
- Social
- Visual
- Hidden curriculum
- Sensory
- Motivation
- Behavior
- Transition
- Siblings or other students

SUPPORT	STRATEGY	DESIRED OUTCOME
Waiting plan		
Communication		
Social		
Visual		
Hidden curriculum		
Sensory		
Motivation		
Behavior		
Transition		
For sibling or other students		
Additional activities for school:		
Additional activities for home:		
REWIND		

In the following pages, these critical areas of support are further defined as they relate to ASD, and strategies specific to each are suggested. (More complete information about each strategy and additional resources for each are provided in the Appendix.)

Each Blueprint also includes boxes for listing additional activities for home and school, designed to help familiarize the child with routines, supports, equipment, or materials that he might encounter during the specific event. This allows the adults in the school, home, and community to collaborate and be consistent in their use of supports, strategies, and instruction across settings.

Finally, the REWIND component serves as a review of the event after its completion. Even with the best planning, not all outings are successful every time. The REWIND box is designed as a place on the Blueprint for making notes about what went well and what could be changed or adapted for another similar outing in the future.

How to Get Started

The Blueprint should be filled out prior to an event. From a teacher planning for an upcoming field trip to the zoo, to a mom preparing to take her children to the public library, or a Scout leader getting ready for the yearly camping trip, the Blueprint provides a structure that highlights the areas where children with ASD most often need support. The persons planning the outing can collaborate in identifying the supports for each area of need and then fill out the Blueprint. Not all tools will be used or filled in for each child or for every setting. Once the tools and the identified supports have been selected and completed, the Blueprint can be utilized *before* the outing as preparation, *during* the outing as a support, and *after* the outing as a review of what went well and what should be done differently the next time.

THE TOOLS

In the following, we will introduce a series of tools that may be used, based on the child's individual needs, for each area of the Blueprint. As mentioned, more detailed information about each tool may be found in the Appendix for ease of adaptation and implementation.

Waiting Plan

Like all of us, children will inevitably have to wait at one point or another, and this can pose challenges. Waiting time is not easily predicted, or if predicted, not always accurate. Because individuals with ASD have an innate need for routine, changes and uncertain outcomes, including time, are very difficult for them to tolerate. However, whether it is 30 seconds or 30 minutes, when the child with ASD is well supported during a period of waiting, it creates a foundation for success by establishing some predictability, thereby keeping the level of anxiety from rising. It is much easier for a child with ASD to wait when he is given some sort of predictability in terms of a countdown or other indicator.

Below are several strategies to help set the parameters for a waiting plan. Overall, it is important that whenever a child has to wait, she is engaged in a motivating, sensory-regulating activity versus simply sitting idle. Such activities may include reading a book, listening to music, spinning a string, or playing a quick game of "I Spy."

- **5, 4, 3, 2, 1 plan** – an adult-directed visual countdown, primarily used for longer periods of time (5-30 minutes).

- **First ... Then ...** – statement that helps to predict that waiting will end and that there is a second step.

- **Single wait card** – a visual cue card handed to the child to signal that she has to wait for a short period of time (no more than 5 minutes).

- **Timers** – a visual countdown that allows the child to independently watch the wait time decrease.

Communication

Communication difficulties are one of the triad characteristics of ASD; as a result, most children need built-in supports in order to communicate effectively. These vary, depending upon the specific needs of the child in both expressive and receptive language areas; often one of these two areas is stronger than the other.

The following strategies utilize the child's strengths in building upon his current level of communication.

- **Augmentative alternative communication (AAC) device** – an electronic voice-output system that may be programmed with single words and/or multi-word sentences; typically used by children with limited verbal skills.

- **Communication board** – a flat, one-page visual prompt that displays the targeted vocabulary, specific to the activity or place with which the child interacts. The child uses the board to interact with others by pointing to each icon to make a sentence or question (expressive language); communication is best received (receptive language) by the child if others involved in the conversation use the board to communicate also.

- **Scripting** – providing complete and/or fill-in-the-blank sentences to prompt the child through an interaction.

- **Verbal prompting** – providing the child with an initial verbal cue to assist him in formulating or completing a sentence.

- **Cue cards** – providing the child with a visual cue to assist her in formulating or completing a question or a comment.

Social

Social skills, another critical area for children with ASD, are supported by both direct instruction of skills (specifically and purposefully teaching a skill to the child) and interpretation of interactions (helping the child understand a social interaction). Most children with ASD must be directly taught social interaction skills because they do not inherently absorb them from the environment. Even when children are successful in making a social exchange, they still may need support in interpreting that exchange. For example, when greeting a peer, a child with ASD may know what to say, but may not understand the response if the peer uses slang terms or figurative speech. By having social supports in place to review the interaction, the child is better able to interpret the details, which helps him to understand the overall context of the encounter, which in turn makes for more successful interactions.

Direct Instruction – Before the Event

- **Social narrative** – written by an adult from the child's perspective about a specific social encounter. It highlights several details within that social situation; child may be involved in the writing process.

- **Role-playing** – involves acting out a social situation as a way to allow the child to practice needed skills prior to the interaction occurring; provides an opportunity to rehearse a variety of potential outcomes through questioning and predicting possible solutions.

- **Priming** – introduction of a social situation prior to its occurrence in order to reduce stress and anxiety. It allows time for processing the situation and predicting possible outcomes to increase success within the interaction.

Interpretation – After the Event

- **Social autopsies** – framework that guides the child to identify a social error she has committed, determine who was impacted by the error, choose what could be done to correct the error, and explore what to do in the future when the child encounters similar situations.

- **Cartooning/comic stripping** – breaks down a social encounter into action pieces by using a comic strip format in which drawings and narrations tell a visual story of the encounter that occurred.

Sample Comic Strip

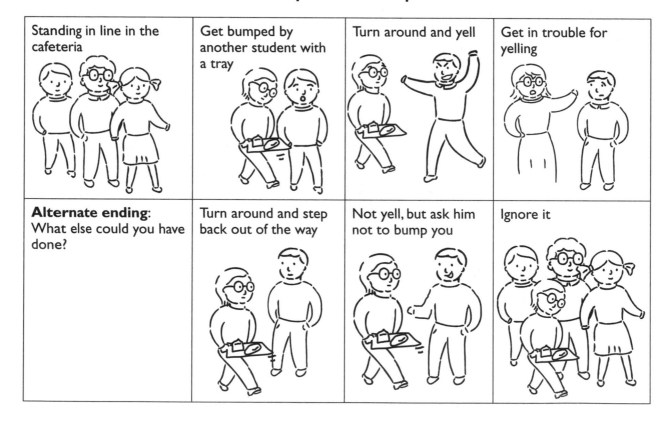

- **SOCCSS (Situation-Options-Consequences-Choices-Strategies-Simulation)** – enhances problem-solving skills through a sequential approach by outlining the experienced encounter, guiding the child to understand the cause-effect relationship and recognize that he has some control over the outcome of the situation according to the decisions he makes.

Visual

Visual supports are highly effective and beneficial for all children with ASD. Visuals help children to better understand an unfamiliar situation or environment by providing concrete, sequential steps and expectations along the way. They also provide support to a verbal direction by physically depicting the thought, idea, or request being expressed verbally. The use of visuals is not necessarily linked to the child's level of verbal communication skills.

Visuals allow the child to picture the request or direction being given verbally, as a way to help her better process the information. In addition to facilitating processing, visual supports allow the child to predict next steps, organize information, express thoughts, make choices, and understand expectations and consequences. Visuals appear in the form of objects, photographs, pictures, symbols, signs, and written words.

- **Schedule/flip book** – defines a plan for the month, week, day, or single event; the number of visuals used and the amount of time displayed is individually determined by each child's needs and use of the schedule; may be created as individual icons attached to a ruler or as a flip book, displaying only one picture per page.

- **Choice makers/reward book** – allows the child to differentiate and select a preferred item.

- **Graphic organizers** – allow the child to better understand concepts by visually highlighting important ideas or steps in relationship to one another.

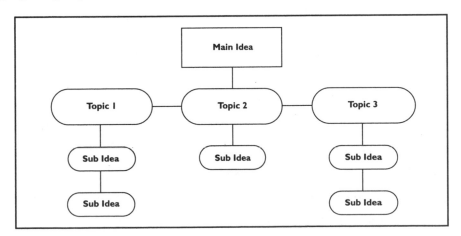

- **Timers** – allows the child to see the time decrease and anticipate a transition.

Hidden Curriculum

The "hidden curriculum" is defined as those unwritten social rules that most people pick up intuitively, such as refraining from picking at body parts in public places, speaking quietly in a doctor's office, or reacting appropriately whether winning or losing a game. Children with ASD do not generally absorb these "rules" through observation or subtle cues and must, therefore, be directly taught. The hidden curriculum is a part of almost every interaction or event, and though it could fall under social supports, it has been given its own place on the Blueprint because it needs to be addressed for each situation. That is, the hidden curriculum should be directly taught for the particular events in which the child will be engaging.

General Considerations for Teaching the Hidden Curriculum

- Age of child
- Culture
- Gender of child
- Specific environment
- Others present

Specific Target Areas for Teaching the Hidden Curriculum

- Social interaction
- Social interpretation
- Facial expressions and body language
- Idioms and metaphors

Sensory

Sensory supports assist the child in first modulating and regulating incoming information through the different senses, then in interpreting and organizing that information, and finally in formulating an appropriate response to the sensory stimuli. Using the sense of hearing as an example, consider that in order to function smoothly in the classroom, the child needs to be able to differentiate between the various sounds, such as children chattering, the teacher giving instruction, chairs squeaking, and the air conditioner humming, and choose to attend to the teacher's voice for instruction rather than to any of the other sounds in the room. Identifying whether a child is hypersensitive (overresponsive) or hyposensitive (underresponsive) to stimuli will assist in providing the appropriate support.

- **Break cue** – a signal that the child can easily and quickly show to indicate that he needs a break or period of time-out.

- **Regulating item** – an item that assists a child in calming or redirecting her sensory system. This may involve wearing headphones or sunglasses, carrying a heavy backpack, or having a weighted blanket across her lap.

- **Stimulus item** – an item that excites or revs up a child's sensory system. This may include holding a textured ball, chewing gum, or standing (instead of sitting) to complete a task.

Motivation

Motivation refers to something that encourages the child to attend to or perform tasks or engage in certain behaviors. For example, an incentive may be offered in advance of completing a task, such as tangible rewards (e.g., stickers, favorite snack). Motivators may also be used to capture the child's attention by developing a relationship between the task to be performed and the child's special interest.

- **Power Card** – a portable, index-sized card with a graphic and three to five statements based upon a simple story written from the perspective of the child's special interest.

- **Motivators in Action (MIA)** – using a child's special interest in an interactive manner within the pre-established context for the particular character, such as hunting for Waldo from *Where's Waldo* or finding blue paw prints in various places to come to a conclusion as in *Blue's Clues*.

Behavior

A behavior support encourages desired behaviors within a given situation so that the child can focus on accomplishing the requested task. The goal is to *regulate* behaviors instead of modifying or extinguishing them. For example, if proper voice volume is a problem, tell the child that she can talk only in a specific area (modify) versus not talking at all (extinguish). Modifying the volume is a much more proactive and meaningful support.

- **Token system** – obtaining a pre-determined number of tokens (e.g., stars, stickers, coins) for performing a desired behavior, which are then exchanged for a reward chosen by the child; used in a short time frame (hourly or just for the morning portion of the day). Rewards can be tiered, requiring a higher number of tokens to be earned for a more desirable reward.

- **5-point scale** – a visual support that modulates a behavior by breaking it into five sublevels. It gives a quantitative, concrete value to each level of behavior, thus allowing the child to evaluate her current level of conduct and alter her behavior or response according to what is best for the given situation.

- **First … Then** … – draws a connection between completing a required task and moving toward a more preferred activity; is presented to the child before starting the original task; can be used with a child repeatedly, but should only be presented as a pair and not as a sequence of events.

Name: Colton		My Control	Scale
Rating	Looks like	Feels like	I can *try* to
5	Kicking or hitting	My head will probably explode	Call my mom go home
4	Screaming at people Almost hitting	Nervous	Go to see Mr. Peterson
3	Quiet sometimes rude talk	Bad mood grumpy	Stay away from kids (The ones I don't like!)
2	Regular kid – not weird!	Good	Enjoy it while it lasts
1	Playing hockey	A million bucks $	Stay that way!

29

From *The Incredible 5-Point Scale*, (p. 29), by K. D. Buron and M. Curtis, 2003, Shawnee Mission, KS: Autism Asperger Publishing Company. Used with permission.

Transition

Because children with ASD characteristically do not respond positively to abrupt change, it is important to provide transition supports that forewarn them about the end of one activity and the beginning of another. Such forewarning gives the child time to process or predict that change is coming and allows her to better anticipate the disruption or closure of the activity in which she is engaged. "Transition cues" may be given verbally, visually, or in tangible form.

- **5,4,3,2,1** or **countdown** – an adult-directed visual countdown, primarily used for longer periods of time (5-30 minutes); may be given verbally or visually.

- **Visual schedule/flip book** – defines a plan for the month, week, day, or single event; the number of visuals used and the length of time they are displayed is individually determined by each child's needs and use of the schedule; may be created as individual icons attached to a ruler or as a flip book, displaying only one picture per page.

- **Collection of item** – providing the child with a list of items or a card of predetermined spaces, all of which must be collected or filled in to signify the completion of an event.

- **Auditory alarm/visual cue** – a predetermined signal that cues the child that only a few minutes of an activity remain and that the conclusion is near; may be a timer, a wristwatch alarm, a flicker of lights, a hand signal or an icon appropriate for the situation and understood by the child.

Siblings or Additional Students

This tool refers to supports provided for siblings or other students, as opposed to using the siblings and students as a support to the child. Providing siblings and students with information about how to help their peer or sibling participate in the outing or prepare for the event in advance allows them to express thoughts and feelings, ask questions, and help make decisions for the outing. This type of supports acknowledges the interests of the sibling or other students, and gives information about the needs, supports, and routines that may be necessary during a particular outing.

- **Share information about the selected supports** – allows the children to be acquainted with and to understand the function of the support.

- **Incorporate the support for all the children** – adapts a support to be universally used with all the students/children in a given environment or situation, such as all the children using a picture BINGO card to identify animals at the zoo.

- **Define a role of the other children** – identifies for the children their specific role in the encounter, which allows them not only to understand their function but also how to engage with the children with ASD.

Additional Home and School Supports

By providing additional supports at home and school, an outing may be broken down into a number of concepts to be introduced, practiced, and experienced in a safe environment ahead of time. This allows the child to slowly explore, manipulate, ask questions, comprehend and then generalize the behaviors and skills needed to participate in the given outing. This extra level of support exposes the child to skills across environments prior to the actual event occurring, and therefore allows her to gain multiple perspectives and form expectations, making the event more predictable.

THE BLUEPRINT IN ACTION

The following examples are grouped into categories that represent places and situations that children may encounter during typical community outings. The examples demonstrate how the Blueprint can be used in a variety of settings for children with different diagnoses, differing levels of needed supports, and of varying ages. For each community event, the individual with ASD may participate with peers, siblings, adults, or a combination of each. The Blueprint should make accommodations for the varying audiences with whom the child may participate. (Please note that each of the tools recommended in the previous chapter are in boldface for easier recognition.)

Note. The list of categories is in no way exhaustive. Users of the Blueprint are encouraged to implement it when preparing for any community outing.

Recreational Activities

Recreational activities include environments such as the bowling alley, an amusement park, a movie theater, a sporting event, the zoo, or the swimming pool.

Going Bowling – Caleb

Caleb is 14 years old and in the ninth grade. His primary diagnosis is high-functioning autism. He also is diagnosed with anxiety disorder and obsessive compulsive disorder. Caleb spends time in both a cross-categorical resource room and general education classes during the day.

Caleb's favorite class is his technology lab class. Caleb loves to work with computers and all different types of technology (e.g., palm pilots). One of his favorite things to do during leisure time is to read the manuals for various models of palm pilots.

For an end-of-the-year bowling trip for physical education class, Caleb's resource room teacher, Mr. Johnson, created a Blueprint. Caleb was placed on a team with three other students from his class.

Prior to the trip, Mr. Johnson and Caleb wrote a **social narrative** about the bowling trip. The narrative was written in paragraph form on one sheet of paper. Caleb had access to the social narrative at the bowling alley if needed. A few days before the outing, Mr. Johnson met with Caleb to go over situations that could occur on the field trip, and talked about appropriate ways to respond to them.

To occupy Caleb while he was waiting his turn to bowl, Mr. Johnson gave him a **manual** for the **electronic bowling scoreboard**, which he obtained from the management. He encouraged Caleb to read the directions aloud to his peers who were waiting to take their turns. When it was nearing Caleb's turn to bowl, Mr. Johnson provided a **countdown** of how many bowlers were left to bowl before it was his turn.

Because Caleb sometimes becomes overwhelmed in large groups or in loud environments, Mr. Johnson brought a variety of supports to assist Caleb if he became anxious. Using a **5-point scale** visual, Caleb was able to self-monitor the volume of his voice. He also had **calming cards** that consisted of activities and exercises that he could do if he became overwhelmed with the environment (i.e., take three deep breaths, close your eyes and slowly count to 10). If needed, he also had a **break card**, a visual cue he was used to carrying with him at school, that he could show his physical education teacher to indicate that he needed to remove himself from the bowling alley and go outside for a few minutes. Caleb's behavior was maintained by providing the above supports.

Because the field trip had been planned several weeks in advance, Mr. Johnson was able to meet with Caleb's physical education teacher to discuss what supports Caleb would need in order to participate successfully in the outing. In addition, Mr. Thomas, the physical education teacher, shared with the other students in Caleb's class some of the supports that Caleb would be using so that he could successfully participate in the field trip. Mr. Johnson also asked Caleb's older brother, who attends the same high school and who went on the field trip the year before, **to talk with Caleb about the trip** and to sit and watch a **videotape** of a popular sitcom that included an episode of bowling.

When Mr. Thomas returned to school the next day, he reviewed the Blueprint with Mr. Johnson to evaluate what had gone well and what had not gone so well. Mr. Johnson realized after the fact that he had not prepared Caleb for the possibility of a malfunction with the electronic bowling scoreboard. Because Caleb became very upset when the scoreboard would not work correctly, Mr. Johnson sat with Caleb and completed a **social autopsy** on the situation.

CALEB

SUPPORT	STRATEGY	DESIRED OUTCOME
Waiting plan	Provide access to written directions on how to operate the electronic scoreboard	Calm behavior while waiting turn; learn the scoring program to assist peers if needed
Communication		
Social	Use social narrative about bowling; priming for events that could possibly occur at bowling alley; social autopsies	Information gained about the environment and situations that may arise; understand expectations
Visual		
Hidden curriculum	Prepare reminders for using a public restroom	Socially appropriate behavior

Sensory	Provide calming cards for when touched accidentally; take a break card	Self-regulation and reduction of anxiety
Motivation	Use Motivators in Action (MIA) – technology	Appropriate behavior while waiting turn to bowl
Behavior	Use 5-point scale to assist with volume control of voice	Use of appropriate volume when speaking
Transition	Implement verbal countdown of how many more people before his turn to bowl	Smooth transition from waiting for turn to bowl to actual time when it is his turn
For sibling or other students	Talk about Caleb's needs and strategies to help him at the bowling alley	Appropriate support provided by peers; acceptance of Caleb as team member

Additional activities for school:
Write and read several times social narrative about bowling trip; use priming activities to prepare for possible situations (e.g., loudness, losing, equipment malfunctions)

Additional activities for home:
Watch bowling show on TV; older brother talk to Caleb about bowling trip and what to expect

REWIND

Social autopsy on situation of malfunctioning scoreboard

At the Zoo – Charlie

Charlie is a bright-eyed 4-year-old diagnosed with Asperger Syndrome. He is very active and enjoys building with Legos and blocks, playing the pots-and-pans band, and looking at books or pictures of animals. Charlie is home schooled and attends a playgroup of other preschoolers with his mother, Gwen, one day a week. During playgroup, Charlie typically engages in parallel play near the other children. He builds elaborate cities out of blocks and purposefully drives his car through them to knock them down while creating a story. If another child spontaneously enters his play, Charlie becomes irritated. However, if the child is introduced with a specific role, such as driving a fire truck that quickly will put out the fire in the building, the scenario about which Charlie just screamed out loud suddenly changes. Charlie allows the child to sit and play, but often does not interact with him in the play sequence. Also, Charlie might not acknowledge that the fire truck is coming to the rescue and may knock it down. The other child might continue to extinguish the fire, while Charlie has moved on to another building to play.

Next week, the playgroup will be taking a field trip to the zoo, including a picnic lunch and time at the playground. Gwen fills out a Blueprint to make sure she has covered all the areas where Charlie needs support so he can fully enjoy his outing.

Gwen created a **book of faces (digital pictures)** and names of all the children in the playgroup. She and Charlie **review the pictures** frequently, talking about each child. Charlie has begun recognizing and naming more of the children during the playgroup.

In addition to reviewing the book, specifically mentioning each child going to the zoo, Gwen adds **pictures of zoo animals** that Charlie will likely see. Using a series of **sentence starters with pictures** that prompt Charlie to ask questions or make a comment, Gwen uses the prompts to make conversation about each child or animal as they look through the book. Gwen uses the same pictures of the zoo animals to make a **BINGO card** that Charlie, and the other children if desired, can use while they travel through the zoo. This serves as a **motivator** to see more animals and to cross them off as they find them, as well as a **predictor** of the number of animals left to find before they leave the zoo. Gwen also wrote a **social narrative** detailing the sequence of events. Knowing that Charlie loves animals and that it might be difficult for him to leave the zoo to have lunch at the playground, Gwen specifically mentioned that when the **BINGO card** was full, it was time to leave for the next activity. By using a **1,2,3 schedule of First zoo ... Then lunch, Then playground**, Charlie was able to anticipate, and thus better cope with, the transition from each activity.

While at the zoo, Charlie used his sentence starters to hand out BINGO cards to the other children and comment about the animals as they were found. He was able to initiate toward the others and interact with them because of the supports he received from his mom and her advanced preparation.

CHARLIE

SUPPORT	STRATEGY	DESIRED OUTCOME
Waiting plan		
Communication	Write out sentence starters pertaining to animals – questions and comments	Engaging with the other children
Social	Review pictures of other children's faces and names; prime with social narrative about events of the day	Recognizing who he is with
Visual	Schedule with sequence of events – zoo, lunch, playground	Predicting next activity
Hidden curriculum		
Sensory		

Motivation	Collect stickers on his zoo BINGO card; see the animals	Going through the zoo with the other children, easily moving from one animal to another
Behavior	Prime with social narrative about events of the day	Knowing what to expect and how to respond
Transition	Explain that full BINGO card equals time to go; visual schedule with sequence of events – zoo, lunch, playground	Advanced warning of leaving zoo; visually predicting next activity
For sibling or other students	Bring zoo BINGO cards for all the children	Including everyone

Additional activities for school:

Additional activities for home:
Review social narrative, pictures of children's faces, books about zoo animals

REWIND

"Hanging out" with Friends – Malik

Malik is 13 years old and diagnosed with Asperger Syndrome. He is in all general education classes, including two honors courses for math and science. He enjoys computers, building with Legos, playing chess, and working complex math equations. In groups he is often the mediator, interpreting what others are trying to say and coming up with a compromise. He is a good friend and a hard worker. Malik is thoughtful in his speech, often taking a long time and using a lot of words to communicate his thoughts; as a result, he often loses his peers' attention. He has an advanced vocabulary and an intelligent perception of many concepts, but has difficulty communicating an idea in a concise manner. Typically, he is able to navigate a social encounter with minimal difficulty interpreting or relating to his peers. However, though Malik is well liked, he often does best in social situations that do not require much verbal expression from him.

Malik wants to hang out with a few of his friends on the weekend. His dad suggests that he invite a couple of them to see the new Indiana Jones movie. He knows that watching a movie together with friends requires limited actual social exchange, but still allows Malik to participate in an activity with his friends. He mentally reviewed the points of the Blueprint as he prepared Malik to invite his friends.

Malik's father **primed** him about the events that would take place – picking up his friends, being dropped off at the movie theater, purchasing tickets, watching the movie, hanging out afterward while waiting to be picked up, and dropping his friends off on the way home. They **scripted the various scenarios**, coming up with conversation topics, questions, and possible concise answers, and then role-played the various events. Malik's dad also covered the **hidden curriculum of going to a movie** with friends. He encouraged his son to be respectful, but still have fun with the guys.

The morning after the show, Malik and his father completed a **social autopsy**, reviewing the details of the interaction, identifying what went well and what should be done differently the next time. Malik was able to articulate specifics about the evening and looks forward to hanging out with his friends again. After the review, Malik's father knows how to better support his son for the next outing and how to prime Malik to continue to self-regulate and make good decisions.

MALIK

SUPPORT	STRATEGY	DESIRED OUTCOME
Waiting plan		
Communication	Script answers to questions	Being concise when responding
Social	Prime for events; role-play interactions, purchasing ticket, etc.	Understanding the sequence of events and the details of each
Visual		
Hidden curriculum	Explain how to act at the movies with friends	Fitting in with the guys
Sensory		
Motivation		
Behavior		
Transition	Create transition cues by priming the interaction (when the movie is over, then ...)	Moving smoothly through the entire interaction
For sibling or other students		

Additional activities for school:

Additional activities for home:
Role-play interactions with peers, purchasing tickets, etc.

REWIND
Complete a social autopsy to determine what went well and what should be done differently the next time

Playing Soccer – Rena

Rena is 10 years old and diagnosed with Asperger Syndrome. She is in a general education classroom with no additional supports. She has difficulty in P.E. because of the large number of students in the class, the noise, and having to follow the unwritten rules of some games. However, she enjoys recess because she gets to kick a soccer ball around the field with no one bothering her. Occasionally, she kicks goals with a few other girls. Rena has three siblings; she enjoys the outdoors, collecting bugs, and watching Mia Hamm play soccer on TV.

When Rena wanted to join the local soccer team, her parents created a Blueprint to ensure that her areas of need were met so that Rena would experience success. They talked with several soccer coaches and chose one they felt would encourage her strengths while understanding her limitations, as well as challenge her to play well and according to the rules. Together, they created a binder of color-coded positions and drills to which Rena could refer during practice. This **graphic organizer** allowed Rena to understand the **sequence** of the drill and the appropriate place to be on the field. It also allowed her to review the drills on her own and gave her a **reference** when she wanted to ask a question.

To support Rena's conduct on the field, her mom wrote a **Power Card** from the perspective of Mia Hamm describing sportsmanlike conduct. She also found a **book at the library** about sportsmanship, rules of playing sports, and being part of a team. Rena understood that not everyone gets to play all of the time. When she was on the sideline, occasionally her coach would have her hold a **wait card** that reminded her that she was part of the team and that her turn would come again soon. Rena's coach often reviewed with the entire team the **hidden curriculum** of both being a good winner and a good loser. The coach and Rena's parents also completed a **SOCCSS** with her, reviewing possible interactions and responses that might come up during practice or a game. They used all these methods for review after a game as well, either to praise Rena's good choices and conduct or to review what reaction could be chosen the next time instead.

To encourage further skill development, Rena often **practiced** playing soccer one-on-one with her dad in the backyard. They would review drills from the binder and practice fundamental skills. On occasion, the entire family would engage in a backyard soccer game, reinforcing the use of Rena's skills in a small controlled group, promoting good sportsmanship, and winning or losing well.

RENA

SUPPORT	STRATEGY	DESIRED OUTCOME
Waiting plan	Use wait card	Understanding she will have another turn again later
Communication	Use graphic organizer	Visually understanding drills and positions
Social	Explain dynamics of being on a team; emphasize sportsmanlike conduct; go over SOCCSS response of interactions; check book out from library on the rules of the game and good sportsmanship	Playing well with others
Visual	Use graphic organizer of drills and positions	Visually understanding drills and positions
Hidden curriculum	Explain how to win or lose well	Positive experience playing on a team
Sensory		
Motivation	Introduce Power Card of Mia Hamm — sportsmanlike conduct	Motivated by favorite player to follow rules of the game and be a part of the team
Behavior	Review SOCCSS for response to interactions	Playing well with others

Transition		
For sibling or other students		

Additional activities for school: Encourage playing at recess; review rules
Additional activities for home: Practice fundamental skills one-on-one; play game with small, controlled group of siblings or friends
REWIND Review SOCCSS, Power Card, hidden curriculum, and positions/drills binder after practice and games to emphasize good choices and better choices — those that could be made the next time instead

Restaurants

There are a variety of restaurant types, including fast food such as McDonald's; sit-down, yet informal chains such as Chili's; and specialty shops such as an ice cream shop or a donut store. Even more formal restaurants such as a special dinner at the country club can be prepared for and supported to ensure a successful experience for all.

Going out for Pizza – Lebrahn

Lebrahn is 12 years old and in the sixth grade. He is diagnosed with autism and uses an assistive technology device or sign language to communicate. In school he is in a self-contained autism classroom and has lunch and gym with his same-aged general education peers. Lebrahn loves to ride on escalators and swing on swings, and likes getting bear hugs from his dad. He also enjoys playing on the computer. Lebrahn's favorite food is pizza and soft drinks. Because he seeks proprioceptive input, deep pressure through the head, his favorite thing to wear is his Colorado Rockies baseball cap. He also enjoys admiring others' baseball hats wherever he goes.

For the upcoming field trip to Mama Mia's Pizza Shoppe with his autism class, Lebrahn's teacher created a Blueprint. Because she knew that Lebrahn loved pizza, Mrs. Stanford brought the **5,4,3,2,1 cards** to count down while Lebrahn waited for his pizza to arrive at the table. She also engaged him in **conversation** with the other students using his **pre-programmed AAC**

device. He was able to use the device to independently order his choice of food as well. In preparation for the outing, his teacher created a **social narrative** using the icons from his AAC device. The narrative was written as a book, highlighting one concept per page. While at Mama Mia's, Lebrahn referred to his **mini-schedule**, created with the same icons, which provided him predictability of each step of the outing. Using a simple "**First Pizza ...Then Video Games**," Lebrahn understood that he would eventually be able to play, but that he needed to eat his pizza first. He was able to respond favorably to the sequence of events because he was given advance notice.

Because Lebrahn sometimes becomes overwhelmed around large groups of people or by loud conversation, his teacher brought a **weighted blanket** that could lie across his lap under the table and two **tennis balls** that could fit on the bottom of the chair legs allowing him to rock. He also had a **break card**, a visual cue he was used to using at school, that he could show his teacher to signal that he wanted to go outside for a couple of minutes. His behavior was maintained by providing adequate sensory input, accessing his communication device, and understanding the concept of "First Pizza … Then Video Games." No additional behavioral supports were identified.

Because the field trip was preplanned, Lebrahn was encouraged to simulate the experience during the week prior to the actual outing. In school, he **role-played** the sequence of events utilizing his AAC device, reviewing the social narrative, and referring to his mini-schedule. At home, he was encouraged to use his AAC device during dinner with his family to **practice** requesting dining items and participating in conversation.

When Mrs. Stanford returned to the classroom after the event, she reviewed the Blueprint to evaluate what had gone well and what needed adjustment for the next trip to Mama Mia's. Because Lebrahn had a difficult time leaving the video games, she emphasized in his social narrative the transition of leaving the video games by highlighting a **transition cue.**

LEBRAHN

SUPPORT	STRATEGY	DESIRED OUTCOME
Waiting plan	Use 5,4,3,2,1 cards; chat with the group	Visual countdown will help cope with waiting
Communication	Use AAC device preprogrammed for outing	Ordering independently
Social	Create social narrative with AAC icons and words — one concept per page	Advance information about environment and expectations of trip
Visual	Prepare single-step cards of event to use while at restaurant	Controlling anxiety and providing predictability
Hidden curriculum	Emphasize reminder phrase: "We do not touch other people's hats"	Keeping hands to himself
Sensory	Bring lap weight to hold while sitting at table; tennis balls for rocking; break card	Self-regulation
Motivation	Remind "First pizza . . . Then video games"	Attending to task
Behavior		
Transition	Add visual icon on daily schedule; use countdown until time to leave	Going and returning with ease
For sibling or other students		

Additional activities for school:
Practice with AAC device; role-play sequence of events

Additional activities for home:
Use AAC device to request and comment on items during dinner

REWIND
Difficult time transitioning from video games when it was time to leave
Suggestion for next time: emphasize transition to leave in social narrative, highlighting transition cue

Stores

This category includes places such as the mall, the grocery store, or the corner pharmacy.

Going to the Mall – Manuel

Manuel is 16 years old and a sophomore in high school. He is diagnosed with Asperger Syndrome. He attends all general education classes with one study skills class in a resource room setting. Manuel loves anything that has to do with football, such as watching football games on television, going to high school football games, reading sports magazines, and playing football video games. This year he volunteered to serve as the water boy for the high school football team.

When working with his resource room teacher, Mr. Baker, Manuel mentioned that he was going to the mall with his brother and some of his brother's friends over the weekend. Mr. Baker created a Blueprint for Manuel to help prepare him. Because he knew that Manuel has difficulty with conversation skills and frequently dominates conversations around topics of interest to him, he decided to use part of the study skills class that day to work on conversational skills.

Mr. Baker used **role-playing** as a way to have Manuel practice interacting with his peers and rehearse ways of participating in situations that could occur at the mall. Manuel and Mr. Baker also created several **scripts** for Manuel to practice so that he would be more comfortable interacting with the guys. In addition, he asked Manuel's brother, who is a senior at the same

school, to **rehearse** the scripts with Manuel at home. A **Power Card** was developed from the perspective of Brett Favre, the quarterback for the Green Bay Packers, emphasizing the need to be a team player when involved in a conversation.

Mr. Baker also shared with Manuel's brother **cue words** that he and his friends could use with Manuel when he started dominating a conversation. Mr. Baker explained to Manuel's brother the importance of including Manuel's **special interest**, football, into the trip to the mall and reminded him to make sure that Manuel had an opportunity to go to the video game store and Lids hat store before leaving the mall.

During another study skills class period that week, Mr. Baker had Manuel watch a **DVD** that included **examples** of students conversing with one another. He and Manuel subsequently discussed the body language portrayed by the students when in conversation, and talked about the various facial expressions of the young adults in the video in order to give Manuel an opportunity to "read" other people's feelings.

Because Manuel easily becomes overwhelmed in crowded places, Mr. Baker and Manuel created several **coping cards** for him to carry when at the mall. The cards consisted of strategies for Manuel to use if he became anxious. Mr. Baker also recommended that Manuel set the **alarm** on his wristwatch for 5 minutes when entering a store of interest, such as Lids, so that when the alarm sounded, he knew it was time to leave the store.

When Manuel arrived at school the following Monday, Mr. Baker asked him how the trip to the mall had gone. Manuel said that it had gone well, but he didn't share any details, which concerned Mr. Baker. When Mr. Baker saw Manuel's brother in the hallway later that day, he asked how everything had gone at the mall. Manuel's brother shared that Manuel became very nervous and agitated when he and his buddies met up with some girls at the food court. Mr. Baker realized that this was an area that he had not discussed with Manuel prior to going to the mall and visited the topic with him the next day during study skills class.

MANUEL

SUPPORT	STRATEGY	DESIRED OUTCOME
Waiting plan		
Communication	Role-play conversations; use scripts	Appropriate conversation; awareness of when dominating conversation
Social	Use social narrative; make cartoon of situations after going to the mall	Information gained about the environment; understanding behavior expectations
Visual		

Hidden curriculum	Use video modeling of others' body language (boredom), conversations/ expressions	Recognizing when dominating conversations
Sensory	Make coping cards	Reduction in stress/ anxiety
Motivation	Incorporate a stop at Lids hat store and the video store; use Power Cards with Brett Favre	Patience and acceptance of peers' areas of interests
Behavior		
Transition	Set timer on wrist watch	Recognizing when it is time to leave stores of interest
For sibling or other students	Share "cue" words with peers to give Manuel when not reading facial/body language	Appropriate support provided by peers; future invitations to go to mall again

Additional activities for school:
Role-playing; video modeling; preparing older brother with strategies to help Manuel

Additional activities for home:
Rehearse scripts with family members

REWIND
Rehearse how to interact with girls at the mall

Going to the Store – Kerrie

Kerrie is 11 years old and in the fifth grade. She is diagnosed with PDD-NOS and uses a Big Mack switch and photographs to make simple requests. In school she is in a self-contained classroom for children with multiple disabilities, but has lunch and recess with same-aged general education peers. Kerrie loves to look at magazines. Her favorite magazine is *American Girl.* She also enjoys listening to music and playing on the playground equipment, especially the slide. Kerrie loves chocolate chip cookies.

In order for Kerrie to be prepared to go to the grocery store to buy the necessary items for the food her class would be cooking that week, her teacher used a Blueprint. Miss Jones, Kerrie's teacher, had prepared a **social narrative** with photographs about the trip to the grocery store. The narrative was written as a book, highlighting one concept per page. Miss Jones and Kerrie began reading the social narrative a few days in advance of the trip, and also read it again right before leaving for the store.

Each child in Kerrie's class is scheduled to go shopping on particular days throughout the month. Miss Jones began preparing Kerrie for the outing several days in advance. For example, she made sure that Kerrie **practiced** buying snack items from the snack counter at school using her photographs. She also sent a book home with Kerrie entitled ***Going to the Grocery Store*** and requested that her family read the book to her several times.

Because Miss Jones knew that Kerrie is constantly picking up things off the floor/ground, she gave Kerrie a **fidget** to carry while walking to the store. When they arrived at the store, Miss Jones gave Kerrie a piece of licorice to **chew** on and prompted her to get a **shopping cart to push**. Both items provided Kerrie with the needed sensory input.

While at the grocery store, Miss Jones assisted Kerrie in using a **photograph grocery list** consisting of the items she would be buying from either the deli or the bakery. Kerrie's responsibility was to hand each photograph representing the item to be purchased to the cashier. Miss Jones built reinforcement into Kerrie's tasks by making sure that the last item to purchase on her list was **chocolate chip cookies**. Also, by using **First Grocery Shopping ...Then Playground,** Kerrie understood that she would eventually be able to play on the playground at school but first needed to buy the items for cooking class. With the use of the concept of First Grocery Shopping ...Then Playground, sensory strategies, and the motivator – chocolate chip cookies – Kerrie was able to purchase all the food items from her list. However, when they had reached the end of the list, Kerrie was agitated and ready to leave the store.

When Miss Jones returned to the classroom, she reviewed the Blueprint to evaluate what had gone well and what adjustments were needed for future trips to the grocery store with Kerrie. She determined that there were too many items on the grocery list for Kerrie to purchase before receiving chocolate chip cookies, and noted the adjustment for future shopping trips in the REWIND section of the Blueprint.

KERRIE

SUPPORT	STRATEGY	DESIRED OUTCOME
Waiting plan	Hold item in hand to keep from reaching for items on ground (leaves, snow) while walking to the store	Hands (sensory needs) regulated
Communication	Use photographs – hand photograph of desired item, Big Mack with photograph or object velcroed	Ordering items at deli and bakery departments for sandwiches (e.g., cheese/bologna/cookies)
Social	Create social narrative with use of photographs – one concept per page	Gaining advance information about environment and expectations of trip
Visual	Photograph grocery list of items to buy at store	Providing predictability and sequence of events
Hidden curriculum		

Sensory	Chew piece of licorice; push cart with assistance	Self-regulation
Motivation	Make chocolate cookies the last item on schedule to buy; use First ... Then board of First grocery shop ... Then playground, or magazine	Attending to task; following schedule to completion to purchase items
Behavior	First ... Then board; sensory strategies, such as licorice, shopping cart, fidget	Maintaining appropriate behavior in grocery store
Transition		
For sibling or other students		

Additional activities for school:
Practice ordering items at snack counter with photographs
Read social narrative about going to the grocery store

Additional activities for home:
Read picture book made by teacher about going to the grocery store

REWIND
After evaluating trip, determination made to reduce the number of items to purchase before receiving reinforcement. Kerrie became agitated after four items; she was required to purchase seven items before getting to request cookies from bakery.

Appointments

All children will need to go to appointments, such as going to the dentist, the pediatrician, the eye doctor, or getting a haircut.

At the Dentist – Preston

Preston, a 3-year-old diagnosed with high-functioning autism, goes to preschool three days a week. The other two days, he is at home with his mom and younger brother. Preston enjoys playing with trains and puzzles, opening and closing doors, and is generally very active. He is verbal and initiates many comments on his own. However, he often needs a verbal prompt to assist his thoughts in response to a question. He plays well with his siblings and the children in his preschool class and interacts with adults who are familiar and introduced as "safe." Preston overwhelms easily in new situations, when around new people, or if he does not understand the sequence of events. He prefers routine and needs clear directions and a plan in advance of activities.

When Lisa, Preston's mother, made his dental appointment, she filled out a Blueprint to help her predetermine areas where Preston would need support during the visit. She was able to **clarify the procedure**, as well as Preston's needs, with the dental office prior to their arrival.

At home, Lisa read a **book about Dora the Explorer going to the dentist**. This enabled Preston to see cartoon pictures of typical dental equipment and the procedure of being at the dentist's office and to review the pages of the book at his own pace as often as he wanted. Because Preston liked the character Dora, the book kept his attention. His mother brought the book to the dentist's office to review again.

When they arrived, the dentist gave Preston a **book of pictures of the actual dentist office**. He was able to review the pictures and compare them to his Dora book while he was still in the waiting room. Lisa also brought a set of **5,4,3,2,1 cards** for the waiting room so that, in addition to the picture review, she and Preston could put together puzzles, counting down the time until it was Preston's turn with the dentist.

Preston was able to hold the **book of pictures** throughout his visit. As he walked into a new room, his mom prompted him through the pictures, flipping the pages as they were completed, and counting down the steps until they were finished. Preston matched the dental equipment to the pictures in his Dora book and understood that he was going to get his teeth looked at and brushed by the dentist just like Dora.

In the dental room, Preston was able to **sit on his mom's lap** while in the dental chair. His mom kept **her arms around him** in a hugging position, helping to make Preston comfortable. The dentist also gave him the **weighted x-ray apron** to wear throughout his time in the chair to add some sensory input and help him relax. His mom brought a **view finder** with a series of slides of characters she knew Preston preferred, such as Thomas the Tank Engine, Blue's Clues, and Bob the Builder. Lisa brought not only the slides Preston had already seen, but also new ones in order to hold his attention throughout the teeth cleaning. As the dentist was looking in Preston's mouth, Preston's attention was directed at looking into the view finder.

Because of the communication between the dental office and Lisa before the appointment, supports were put into place in advance to welcome and comfort Preston during his visit. After the conclusion of his teeth cleaning, the dentist let Preston choose a toy out of the **prize box** as a reward.

PRESTON

SUPPORT	STRATEGY	DESIRED OUTCOME
Waiting plan	Use 5,4,3,2,1 cards; work puzzles in the waiting room	Occupied while waiting for dentist
Communication		
Social		
Visual	Use flip book with photos of various steps	Visually predicting sequence of events

Hidden curriculum		
Sensory	Use weighted x-ray vest; held by mother	Able to sit still and feel comforted because of deep pressure and secure feeling from mom
Motivation	Bring view finder; MIA: Dora book of parallel story — compared story to real experience	Visualized distraction to take focus off of mouth; predicting sequence of events paralleling a favored (motivating) character
Behavior		
Transition	Flip pages of book to see next step	Visually predicting sequence of events
For sibling or other students		

Additional activities for school:

Additional activities for home:
Read "Show Me Your Smile!: A Visit to the Dentist" (Dora the Explorer) by Christine Ricci and Robert Roper "
Become familiar with view finder

REWIND

Public Places

These include environments such as religious services, the public library, the post office, and the police or fire station.

Attending Religious Services – Carter

Carter is 8 years old and diagnosed with autism. He is nonverbal and communicates through sign language and, at school, with an AAC device as well. He is in a self-contained special education classroom. Carter is mild-mannered, very outgoing and attentive to others, and enjoys pointing out people that he recognizes. He loves music, watching monkeys at the zoo, and going to his grandmother's house after school.

Carter's family attends church each Sunday morning. Carter has a **one-on-one buddy**, Julie, who accompanies him to Sunday school. Together with Julie, his parents created a Blueprint to ensure that all Carter's areas of need were well supported.

Carter is responsive to verbal directions, but Julie was able to also use **sign language** to visually communicate signs with Carter that he would recognize. When needed, she also **sketched line drawings** of instructions or concepts for him to view. Though Carter was beginning to recognize sight words, he used a **picture Bible** to more easily understand the stories being taught. He was able to participate with the group by pointing to the answer on his picture or signing a reply.

Each week when Carter arrived at Sunday school, Julie had him **point out and greet each student** in the class. The other boys were responsive to his greeting, and they were **prompted** to engage Carter in their activity or conversation. He typically did not have trouble transitioning between activities, seeing each activity (small group, music time, and finding his parents at the end of the morning) as reinforcing in itself. Nevertheless, Julie gave Carter **a cue in advance that transition was approaching** and stayed with him as the group slowly changed locations, prompting him towards the next activity. If he needed a **visual countdown**, she simply used her fingers, slowly lowering one at a time. When all the fingers were down, Carter clearly understood it was time to move.

During small-group time, all the boys played an active game as they reviewed the lesson and sat on the floor in their teams. Therefore, Carter's small leg movement or hand waving were not distractions, nor did they inhibit his ability to participate. During large-group time, all the children sat in chairs; Carter enjoyed choosing his color of chair and staying in it. He danced to the music and signed the words. His parents got him a **CD of the songs** to listen to at home, so he was very familiar with the music and could identify each song as it began. Like all the children, Carter **received tickets** for active participation, which could later be exchanged for prizes. Though Carter needed a little more **space** and had to move more often than most of the other elementary-age students, the overall environment and program were designed to accommodate active elementary students. Therefore, supports for Carter were easily adapted and implemented, which allowed him to fully participate.

CARTER

SUPPORT	STRATEGY	DESIRED OUTCOME
Waiting plan	Count 5,4,3,2,1 on fingers	Waiting for transition
Communication	Use sign language; visual drawings	Understanding what is being said — directions and lesson
Social	Greet classmates; one-on-one buddy	Interacting with peers
Visual	Use picture Bible; line drawings	Understanding what is being said — directions and lesson
Hidden curriculum		
Sensory	Provide space to move	Regulating sensory system and attending to lesson/activity

Motivation	Use system whereby participating equals getting a ticket; dancing to the music	Participating in lesson/ activity
Behavior		
Transition	Use sign language prompt: music, parent, group	Easily moving between activities and rooms
For sibling or other students	Encourage response to greeting and interactions; give them opportunity to initiate toward and include Carter in activities	Receiving a response from peers; encouraging interactions

Additional activities for school:

Additional activities for home:
Listen to music CD at home; review picture Bible

REWIND

Trips

A vacation with family members or a trip with friends may necessitate long car rides, airplane rides, and staying at a relative's house or in a hotel.

Visiting Relatives for the Holidays – Jimmy

Jimmy, 10 years old, is in the fourth grade and has Asperger Syndrome. Jimmy is in a general education classroom all day with same-aged peers. He gets along well with most of his class-mates; however, he has limited peer interaction during lunch and recess. His favorite subject is science, and he really likes dinosaur fossils. When not at school, Jimmy spends most of his time playing video games or riding his bike. He enjoys exploring his neighborhood for lost treasures and playing UNO with his siblings.

Jimmy and his family are traveling to their relatives' house for Christmas. This means Jimmy will encounter a large group of somewhat unfamiliar faces after traveling in the car for six hours. Jimmy's parents created a Blueprint to prepare for the journey.

Jimmy's mom, Sonja, had all three of her children sit down to **create a list of items** they would like to bring in the car to play alone and to play together. Jimmy decided to bring his portable video games, his fossil books, and his magnifying glass. Together, the children decided to bring the UNO cards and a tray so they could play in the car. They also chose to bring a few travel games and some movies for the DVD player.

Sonja created a **visual choice book** for Jimmy by taking digital pictures of his preferred car items and placing them into a small binder. Having a visual when making a choice would allow Jimmy to make an easier decision in case he was getting overwhelmed or bored in the car. Because Sonja knew that Jimmy enjoys exploring the neighborhood for lost treasure, she developed an MIA by **creating a map** highlighting several landmarks they would pass along the way and made the final destination the treasure. Jimmy was able to use the map to mark off the places they were passing and continue to look ahead to finding the treasure.

Before they left, Sonja reviewed the trip with Jimmy. They **drew cartoons** of the events that would occur, including the people who would be present and expectations for each activity. Sonja also discussed the **hidden curriculum** of receiving gifts – attending to others as they opened their gifts and making appropriate responses and comments. They also talked about what might make Jimmy feel overwhelmed and **created a plan for him to take a break** as needed. Jimmy understood that he would not always be allowed to leave a particular event, so he came up with some **relaxation**

routines, such as closing his eyes and counting to 10, that he could implement while staying in his seat. Jimmy also made a **5-point scale** for anxiety so he could cue his mother without using a lot of words. If he became extremely overwhelmed, he could simply hold up five fingers and then begin his relaxation routine. If he was feeling calm, he could signal just one or two fingers to his mother. This worked well because they could communicate across the room without anyone noticing – his mom giving the questioning cue of "How are you?" and Jimmy responding with the appropriate number of fingers.

Together they also created a **family album**, placing a digital picture of each person with his or her name on a separate page. Jimmy was able to ask questions about his relatives and become familiar with them before he would see them. They also discussed possible questions that the relatives might ask Jimmy and what he could say in response. This made him feel much more comfortable.

JIMMY

SUPPORT	STRATEGY	DESIRED OUTCOME
Waiting plan	Make choice book of individual activities	Occupied during ride
Communication	Review possible questions relatives may ask	Understanding questions and making an appropriate response
Social	Use cartooning – who, where, and what	Visually seeing the series of events that will occur, including those who will participate
Visual	Create MIA of a map with landmarks and the final destination like a treasure map	Countdown to arrival
Hidden curriculum	Show pictures of relatives; emphasize saying thank you for gifts	No surprise comments about relatives; appropriate response for if already have gift, do not like gift, etc.

Sensory	Use cue for taking a break from too many people, lots of noise, new smells	Self-regulation before becoming over-stimulated
Motivation	Use MIA: Pirate looking for a treasure – create a map with landmarks and final destination	Countdown to arrival
Behavior	Use 5-point scale for anxiety of relatives	Self-regulating anxiety level, reaction and need
Transition		
For sibling or other students	Review 5-point scale; create list of activities for the car – both group and alone	Empowering siblings
Additional activities for school:		
Additional activities for home: Review pictures of relatives; review cartoons of events; have Jimmy pack special items for the car in his backpack		
REWIND		

Special Events

Going to camp, being invited to a sleepover at a friend's house, or attending a birthday party are special events in children's lives that include important interactions with peers. Other special events may occur with family members such as weddings, funerals, or family reunions.

Going to a Birthday Party – Sebastian

Sebastian is 8 years old and diagnosed with high-functioning autism. He is in a general education classroom at school with no additional supports. He gets along well with friends during structured activities, but has difficulty during recess and in the cafeteria during lunch. Sebastian is an only child and receives a lot of one-on-one attention from his parents at home.

Sebastian was invited to a birthday party for Marco, one of the boys in his class. Frank, Sebastian's dad, created a Blueprint to identify where Sebastian might need support to successfully participate in the birthday party. He first created a **social narrative**, outlining details of the party and how Sebastian might interact or respond, such as when Marco opens birthday gifts, how to participate and wait his turn during the games, and explaining the **hidden curriculum** of a birthday party. He also included **strategies** for Sebastian to choose if the noise or the number of people overwhelmed him. **Safe places, safe people, and safe procedures were identified**. Frank was able to **find pictures** of the venue online when it was decorated for a party. He shared these with Sebastian to give him a **visual perspective of the environment** prior to the party. Together, they also **wrote down and role-played some conversation ideas**. By creating a script in advance and **practicing with his dad**, Sebastian was able to identify a variety of relevant conversation topics that would be interesting to the other boys at the party, too.

Sebastian went to the party and was able to participate with the other boys in games, eating cake, and watching presents being opened. When he felt overwhelmed, he asked Marco's mother if he could **take a break** for a few minutes. He walked away and **counted to 10 and took deep breaths**, and when he was ready, he rejoined the group.

After the party, Frank referred to the **social narrative and pictures** as he listened to Sebastian recall the events of the day. Frank **reinforced good choices** that Sebastian had made and pointed out details of the party by using the same **pictures** he had shown Sebastian to prime him originally.

SEBASTIAN

SUPPORT	STRATEGY	DESIRED OUTCOME
Waiting plan		
Communication	Review script of possible questions to ask others and appropriate responses	Holding a conversation on relevant topics with peers
Social	Develop social narrative detailing events of a birthday party	Identifying details and explaining possible choices and reactions
Visual	View pictures of facility decorated for a birthday party	Lessening initial reaction by providing advanced visual warning of environment
Hidden curriculum	Explain how to celebrate the birthday person	Understanding that the majority of attention will go to the birthday person
Sensory	Review possible stimulators: many people, lots of noise; create plan to de-escalate if needed	Recognizing stimulators and take a break before getting too overwhelmed
Motivation		
Behavior		
Transition		
For sibling or other students		

Additional activities for school:

Additional activities for home:

REWIND
Reviewed the social narrative and pictures, identifying good choices that Sebastian made while at the party

Attending a Family Wedding – Jeremy

Jeremy is 5-1/2 years old and in kindergarten. He is diagnosed with autism. In school, Jeremy is in a self-contained autism classroom but has circle time with same-aged general education peers. He has very limited verbal skills and uses picture symbols to communicate. Jeremy loves Nemo and Mickey Mouse. His favorite snack is gummy bears. He enjoys swinging on swings, looking through photo albums, and hiding under a weighted blanket or beanbag chair. Jeremy has difficulty managing his behavior in crowded and loud environments. He often becomes overwhelmed, at which time he hits others or screams.

Jeremy's mom contacted his teacher, Mrs. Briggs, and asked if she could help prepare Jeremy for his aunt's upcoming wedding. Mrs. Briggs created a Blueprint for the wedding and reception. Mrs. Briggs first wrote a **social narrative** for Jeremy, including photographs of the church, reception hall, Jeremy's aunt and future uncle, and several others that had been provided by Jeremy's mom. She asked Jeremy's mom to read the social narrative to him several times before the day of the wedding. Mrs. Briggs also read it at school and talked about the day's events with Jeremy. She asked Jeremy's mom to contact the bride to find out what food would be served at the reception so that Jeremy would know ahead of time. Since Jeremy loves to look at photo albums, Mrs. Briggs recommended that Jeremy's mom have him look at family members' **wedding albums**.

Mrs. Briggs gave Jeremy's mom a **First ... Then board** to use at both the wedding and the reception. Icons representing wedding and buffet were placed on the "First" side and an icon of gummy bears was placed on the "Then" side. Mrs. Briggs explained how and when to use the First ... Then board. She also made a **visual schedule** for Jeremy to use on the day of the wedding, consisting of icons representing various events of the day.

Because Mrs. Briggs knew that Jeremy often gets upset when he is in loud environments, she gave Jeremy's mother a set of **earphones** to use at the reception. Jeremy was used to wearing them at school. She also encouraged Jeremy's mom to **take him out of the reception hall when the music became loud**. During the ceremony and while he waited for his family's turn to go to the buffet line, Jeremy was given his **Nemo** and **Mickey Mouse** stuffed animals to hold. Mrs. Briggs also let Jeremy's mom borrow one of the classroom **lap weights** so that he could lay it on his lap while eating. Because the reception was a buffet, Jeremy was given an **icon choice board** to communicate to his mom what he wanted to eat.

Jeremy's mom called Mrs. Briggs after the wedding to share with her how the day had gone. She explained that Jeremy did remarkably well and thanked Mrs. Briggs for helping prepare Jeremy for this important family event.

JEREMY

SUPPORT	STRATEGY	DESIRED OUTCOME
Waiting plan	Prepare First ... Then board; hold Nemo/Mickey stuffed animals	Quiet/calm behavior while waiting during ceremony
Communication	Prepare communication board with icons representing wants/needs	Making requests, expressing needs
Social	Use social narrative with photographs of events of wedding	Prepared for events of ceremony/reception
Visual	Prepare icon schedule of events of wedding, choice board of icons for choices for food at reception	Controlling anxiety; understanding events to occur at wedding/reception
Hidden curriculum		
Sensory	Leave reception area when volume was undesirable and return when ready; offer earphones when music too loud, lap weight for dinner	Sensory system regulated

Motivation	Provide Nemo/Mickey Mouse stuffed animals to hold during wedding ceremony	Appropriate behavior during ceremony
Behavior	Use a First ... Then board: "First the required activity ... Then gummy bears"	Completion of various wedding activities with calm behavior
Transition	Use visual icon schedule for transition from one event to another	Smooth transition from one event to another at wedding/reception
For sibling or other students		

Additional activities for school:
Read book/s about weddings

Additional activities for home:
Mom contact bride and ask for menu to prepare Jeremy of foods to be served; read social narrative with photographs of church, reception hall, etc.; look at photo albums of other family members' weddings

REWIND

SUMMARY

Children with ASD should be given the opportunity to participate in age-appropriate activities, just like their peers. By using the Blueprint presented here along with the suggested tools carefully selected for a given child and a given outing, adults work together to help the child generalize skills across settings and in the process build the child's self-confidence. The process highlights the importance of seeing the child with all of his unique characteristics and needs.

By using the Blueprint, preparing ahead of time, and being consistent, adults can help children with ASD participate successfully in all kinds of environments and community activities. Parents, educators, service providers, and community members can feel at ease, no longer hesitate, but encourage the child to participate in various events. Strategies that support their needs and the specific community event help children with ASD experience the world in a whole new way.

APPENDIX

5,4,3,2,1

A 5,4,3,2,1 strip is a transition strategy that is designed to answer the question "How much longer?" an activity will last or "How much longer to wait?" before an activity begins. It provides a simple visual to support a student in making a smooth transition from one event to another.

A 5,4,3,2,1 strip can be made in a variety of ways, from simply writing the numbers on a piece of paper and crossing off one number at a time, to using a premade horizontal or vertical strip with velcroed numbers.

For additional information:

> Hudson, J. (2006). *Prescription for success: Supporting children with autism spectrum disorders in the medical environment.* Shawnee Mission, KS: Autism Asperger Syndrome Publishing Company.

First ... Then

The First ... Then board is a simple visual strategy that provides a child with an understanding of what he must do first and what he will get to do next. A preferred activity is usually the "then" part of the board. For instance, if a child wants to play with a video game, she may "first" have to complete a reading task and "then" get to play with her video game. The board is used as a reference for the child to stay focused on the required activity so that she can receive the preferred item/activity. First ... Then boards can be made using objects, photographs, picture symbols, or words, depending on the child's needs.

Sample First ... Then Board

For additional information:

Hannah, L. (2001). *Teaching young children with autistic spectrum disorders to learn*. London: National Autism Society.

Single Wait Card

A single wait card is a visual support that is handed to a child as a cue that the child needs to wait for a brief period of time. Waiting is an abstract concept and is often difficult for a child with ASD to understand. A wait card helps the child understand that an activity is going to happen but not immediately. The card provides the child with a visual as well as something to hold. A wait card can be used to help a child wait for a turn during a game, wait in line to leave a setting, or wait while the teacher is changing the music CD on the CD player.

It is important not to use a wait card for extended periods of time. Children should be actively engaged in an activity rather than waiting for a lengthy period of time.

Sample Wait Card

For additional information:

> Bondy, A., & Frost, L. (2001). *A picture's worth: PECS and other visual communication strategies in autism.* Bethesda, MD: Woodbine House Publisher.

Time Timer™

A Time Timer™ is a tool that enables a child to tell how much time is left without having to understand how to tell time. The timer is a visual representation of time that has passed. It works by simply moving the red disc on the face counterclockwise to the desired time period. The red shaded section gets smaller and smaller as time passes until no red is visible. When the color red has disappeared, the child is informed that an activity is completed and that it is time to transition to another activity.

For additional information:

> Time Timer Inc. – www.timetimer.com

AAC Device

An augmentative alternative communication (AAC) device is a speech-output device that provides an individual with limited or no speech a "voice." While some AAC devices are quite sophisticated, simple devices are available for children who have not yet mastered identifying pictures and who need a means of communicating their needs and wants. Devices may include switches with a preprogrammed message such as "I want a cookie, please," or a message used in a specific social situation such as "Happy Halloween." Other AAC devices consist of visual symbols and/or words. Many of the more advanced computerized systems also have word-processing capabilities.

For additional information:

> Quill, K. (2000). DO-WATCH-LISTEN-SAY: *Social and communication intervention for children with autism.* Baltimore: Paul H. Brookes.

Communication Board

A communication board is a visual support that consists of vocabulary specific to an activity or place. A communication board gives a child the means of interacting with others by touching key words and/or pictures on the board in order to convey a message. The vocabulary on the board is organized in a left-to-right fashion in order to promote the development of literacy skills. It is important that a communication board be portable and sturdy, allowing the child to carry it from place to place so that it is readily available at all times. A communication board can be used with children who have little to no speech as well as with children who can speak but need support to expand their verbal skills.

Sample Communication Board

For additional information:

Hodgdon, L. (1995). *Visual strategies for improving communication: Practical supports for school and home.* Troy, MI: Quirk Roberts Publishing.

Scripting

Scripting presents a child with a limited number of choices for what to do when involved in certain interactions. A script is written specifically for the particular child and the particular social situation. Scripts may be created with words only or be accompanied by pictures, symbols, or photographs. When a child is in a situation where he has to interact with peers or adults, a script offers ideas for how to respond and supports the development of social skills. Scripts present the child with the words to say or the actions to demonstrate in a given situation.

Sample Script to Use When Meeting Someone for the First Time

1. "Hello, my name is _____."

2. "What is your name?"

3. "Hi, glad to meet you."

For additional information:

> McClannahan, L., & Krants, P. (2005). *Teaching conversation to children with autism: Scripts and script fading.* Bethesda, MD: Woodbine House Publisher.

> Mayo, P., & Waldo, P. (1986). *Scripting: Social communication for adolescents.* Eau Claire, WI: Thinking Publications.

Verbal Prompting

Verbal prompting involves an adult or peer verbally cueing a child to initiate communication or make a response. Depending upon the needs of the child, the verbal prompt may include the initial sound or syllable of a word, known as a *partial verbal prompt,* or a *full verbal prompt* consisting of an entire word or a phrase. For example, if the desired response is for the child to initiate "good morning," the prompt may range from "say 'g …'" to "say 'good morning.'"

For additional information:

> Bellini, S. (2006). *Building social relationships: A systematic approach to teaching social interaction skills to children and adolescents with autism spectrum disorders and other social difficulties.* Shawnee Mission, KS: Autism Asperger Publishing Company.

Cue Cards

Cue cards are communication supports that include one or more messages and that provide a visual of what to say in certain situations; as such, they take the place of verbal prompts. Used more often with verbal children, cue cards can include pictures, symbols, or words. Cue cards can serve as prompts for building conversational skills as well as reminders of how to interact in specific situations. They silently encourage the child to interact. For children who are unable to spontaneously formulate verbal responses due to anxiety around novel or uncomfortable situations, cue cards offer an alternative form of communication.

Sample Cue Card

> # Hello, it is nice to meet you.

For additional information:

> Quill, K. (2000). DO-WATCH-LISTEN-SAY: *Social and communication intervention for children with autism.* Baltimore: Paul H. Brookes.

Social Narrative

A social narrative provides social ideas and rules in a brief story format. The narrative may include pictures, photographs, or words alone, depending upon the child's needs. Narratives may be presented in a book form, with one or two sentences per page, or text may be written on a piece of paper in paragraph form. Social narratives present expectations for particular social situations. Thus, children are given information about a circumstance as well as ideas, examples, or directions for what might happen while in the situation and how to react. Social narratives can help children learn how to manage new or different situations. Whenever possible, children should assist in writing their own social narratives. Social narratives can be read by the child on a one-time basis or be read over and over before an event occurs.

Sample Social Narrative – What Do People Do at the Library?

A library is a place filled with books. Sometimes people go to a library to read books. Sometimes people borrow books from the library. Before taking the books home, they sign the books out with the librarian. Everyone at the library tries to talk quietly. People reading their library books like it when it is quiet. I will try to read my library books with a quiet voice when I visit the library.

For additional information:

> Gray, C. (1995). *Social Stories™ unlimited: Teaching social skills with social stories and comic strip conversations.* Jenison, MI: Jenison Public Schools.

> Gray, C. (1998). *The advanced Social Story™ workbook.* Jenison, MI: Jenison Public Schools.

Role-Playing

Role-playing involves a child acting out or practicing a social interaction or certain skills with an adult and/or peer(s) in a nonthreatening structured environment. The skills being practiced may entail newly introduced skills or behaviors that are reoccurring but need further training. They may also include feared or avoided social situations. A role-play can incorporate both scripted and unscripted situations. During a role-play, children are aided to problem solve and use the most appropriate response to the given situation and practice acceptable behavior. The goal of role-playing is to encourage the child to use the rehearsed skills in future real-life situations.

For additional information:

> Bellini, S. (2006). *Building social relationships: A systematic approach to teaching social interaction skills to children and adolescents with autism spectrum disorders and other social difficulties.* Shawnee Mission, KS: Autism Asperger Publishing Company.

> Coucouvanis, J. (2005). *Super skills: A social skills group program for children with Asperger Syndrome, high-functioning autism and related challenges.* Shawnee Mission, KS: Autism Asperger Publishing Company.

Priming

Priming consists of informing a child of an activity or routine in advance of it happening. This may occur the day or night before, on the day of the event, or immediately prior to an event. Priming is most effective when it is a part of the child's routine. Priming consists of a brief description that overviews the event or routine, specifying the materials needed or steps to be completed. When available, actual materials are introduced or a list of materials needed or steps to the routine are written out for the child to see. Priming gives the child predictability, therefore, reducing stress and anxiety while increasing success.

Sample Priming

"When we get home from school, you will need to finish your homework because we also have to pack your suitcase tonight for our trip tomorrow morning. I know your favorite TV show comes on at 7 P.M., so I want to help you be all done with your homework and packing before it begins."

For additional information:

Myles, B. S., & Adreon, D. (2001). *Asperger Syndrome and adolescence: Practical solutions for school success.* Shawnee Mission, KS: Autism Asperger Publishing Company.

Wilde, L. D., Koegel, L. K., & Koegel, R. L. (1992). *Increasing success in school through priming: A training manual.* Santa Barbara: University of California.

Social Autopsies

A social autopsy is a problem-solving strategy and a visual review of a social interaction. It allows a child to gain an understanding of an interaction, to identify errors and make adjustments for the future.

An autopsy asks the child to: (a) identify the social error in the interaction, (b) name who was harmed or affected by the error, (c) determine an appropriate correction for the error, and (d) consider a plan so the error does not occur in the same situation again. It is important when using a social autopsy to provide immediate feedback and positively reinforce the child as he processes the interaction and problem solves.

For additional information:

Bieber, J. (Producer). (1994). *Learning disabilities and social skills with Richard Lavoie: Last one picked ... first one picked on.* Washington, DC: Public Broadcasting Service.

Myles, B. S., & Adreon, D. (2001). *Asperger Syndrome and adolescence: Practical solutions for school success.* Shawnee Mission, KS: Autism Asperger Publishing Company.

Cartooning/Comic Stripping

In cartooning, a series of line drawings or pictures depict a scenario or encounter. It can be used either in advance of the event or afterwards as a review. Often children with ASD are better able to draw out their thoughts than to tell them in words. To add narration to a cartoon, conversation bubbles may be inserted for each character. Cartooning may be referred to as comic stripping, if several pictures are used in a series to represent steps in an event.

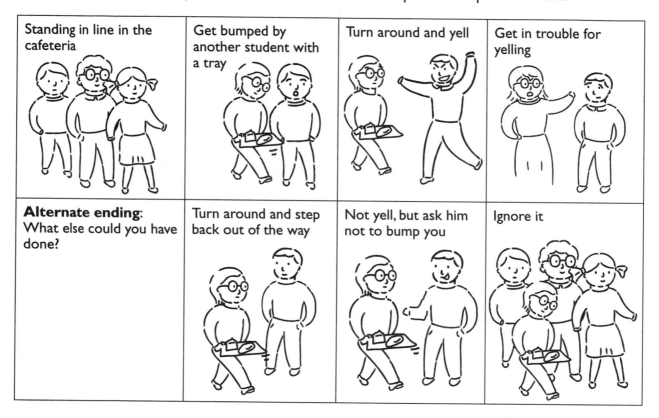

For additional information:

Arwood, E. L., & Kaulitz, C. (2007). *Learning with a visual brain in an auditory world.* Shawnee Mission, KS: Autism Asperger Publishing Company.

Gray, C. (1994). *Comic strip conversations: Colorful, illustrated interactions with students with autism and related disorders.* Jenison, MI: Jenison Public Schools.

Gray, C. (1995). *Social Stories™ unlimited: Teaching social skills with social stories and comic strip conversations.* Jenison, MI: Jenison Public Schools.

SOCCSS

This sequential social problem-solving strategy allows the child to review the cause-and-effect relationship in an interaction and in the process learn that she has influence over her environment and the outcomes of her interactions.

The SOCCSS contains six steps:

(1)   **S**ituation: The child independently recalls the who, what, when, where, and why of the social interaction. The facilitator can prompt for detail if needed.

(2)   **O**ption: The child and facilitator brainstorm and record all options that the child could choose in the identified social interaction.

(3)   **C**onsequences: An outcome is identified for each option previously recorded. Some options may have multiple consequences. The child may need prompting or role-playing to identify a consequence for a particular option.

(4)   **C**hoices: All the option/consequence pairs are prioritized by giving them a numerical value or identifying them as yes/no. Ultimately, the child identifies the top pair that he feels he can carry out to obtain the result that he desires.

(5)   **S**trategies: A plan is developed to carry out the chosen option/consequence. This should be led by the student to facilitate decision making and taking ownership to follow through with the determined plan.

(6)   **S**imulation: The plan is practiced in a safe and controlled environment by writing it out in steps, role-playing, drawing it out in cartoon format, or telling someone else in detail.

For additional information:

Myles, B. S., & Adreon, D. (2001). *Asperger Syndrome and adolescence: Practical solutions for school success.* Shawnee Mission, KS: Autism Asperger Publishing Company.

Visual Schedules

Visual schedules are made of a combination of drawings, photographs, words, or pictures to display a sequence of events for a determined period of time. A schedule may be made for an entire day, one event, a whole week, or for just the morning. The length of time and number of items on the schedule are determined by the needs of the child and the nature of event(s). The schedule should not overwhelm, but give predictability and a plan to reference and follow.

For additional information:

Savner, J. L., & Myles, B. S. (2000). *Making visual supports work in the home and community: Strategies for individuals with autism and Asperger Syndrome.* Shawnee Mission, KS: Autism Asperger Publishing Company.

Choice Makers

This strategy presents visual representations of choices that are available during a predetermined time frame or event. Seeing the options provides a concrete choice of one item and, therefore, not the others. Often, if an open-ended question is presented to a child with ASD, he may not conceptualize the available choices and, therefore, choose by default a choice that previously was selected. By offering a concrete, visual choice, the child is able to make a selection based on knowledge of availability. Further, choices offer predictability and a basis for security and certainty.

This strategy gives the child control and choice over her environment during a series of tasks or events that are considered non-negotiable. By creating a book, a variety of rewards are visually displayed from which the child chooses one and pairs it with the requested tasks. Rewards are chosen prior to starting the tasks; a fun reward is identified and coupled with each step of the event. The purpose of reward books is to provide predictability and incentive for completing tasks, not to create rigidity. If the child prefers to change his reward choice, flexibility should be considered for each specific incident.

Sample Choice Maker

READ A BOOK	PLAY ON THE COMPUTER	DRAW A PICTURE

For additional information:

Hudson, J. (2006). *Prescription for success: Supporting children with autism spectrum disorders in the medical environment.* Shawnee Mission, KS: Autism Asperger Syndrome Publishing Company.

Graphic Organizer

Graphic organizers highlight important information in a way that makes it easier to understand. Visual and systematic, graphic organizers are used to show associations between facts, thoughts, or ideas. They provide concrete links to abstract concepts and may present cause and effect, sequences, or main idea and subtopic relationships.

Sample Graphic Organizer

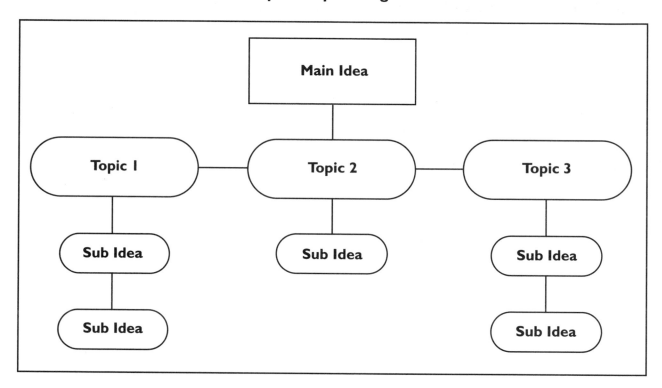

For additional information:

Myles, B. S., & Adreon, D. (2001). *Asperger Syndrome and adolescence: Practical solutions for school success.* Shawnee Mission, KS: Autism Asperger Publishing Company.

Wiig, E., & Wilson, C. (2001). *Map it out: Visual tools for thinking, organizing and communicating.* Eau Claire, WI: Thinking Publications.

Power Card

A Power Card is a simple story written from the perspective of a child's special interest to motivate him to perform a specific behavior. In addition to composing a simple story detailing the desired behavior and motivation, a card is created that outlines three to five behaviors that the special interest wants the child to remember and a visual icon representing the special interest. The card is small and portable, allowing the child to carry it around or place it in significant spots. When the child sees the card or the icon, it triggers the highlighted behaviors and motivates the child to display the desired outcomes.

Sample Power Card

Ray loved NASCAR. He loved it so much that he would speed through the hallways, not looking up to see if there was anyone in his way. He would run into people, and without even stopping to acknowledge the bump, he would speed around them.

To teach Ray to slow down and pay attention, Mr. Rutherford created a Power Card for him using his special interest in NASCAR. He used the perspective of Dale Earnhart, Jr. He described that on the racetrack, Dale drove very fast because he was in a competition, but when he was driving on the road, he followed the speed limit signs and was a very safe driver. Dale encouraged Ray to be very speedy when he was in a competition or in gym class, but if he was in the hallway, at home or school, he warned him to walk at a safe pace to not cause any crashes.

Dale Earnhardt, Jr. wants you to remember these things about being fast:

1. Good times to be very fast are when you are in a competition, outside or in gym class.

2. If you are in the hallway at school or at home, it is important to move at the same pace as others so you do not run into them.

3. It is important to keep your head up and your eyes open as you move through the hallway. This also will help you to avoid a crash.

If you practice these tips, you will be very fast at the right time and avoid getting into a crash.

For additional information:

Gagnon, E. (2001). *Power cards: Using special interests to motivate children and youth with Asperger Syndrome and autism.* Shawnee Mission, KS: Autism Asperger publishing Company.

Motivators in Action

A Motivator in Action (MIA) uses a child's special interest in an interactive manner within the pre-established context for the particular character, such as hunting for Waldo from *Where's Waldo* or finding blue paw prints in various places to come to a conclusion as in *Blue's Clues*. It may also involve using a map to navigate between two points, such as in *Dora the Explorer,* or simply creating a treasure map. However, it is not substituting the child's special interest, such as Pokémon looking for clues or making a map. The use of the character must be preserved. For example, the typical function of the *Where's Waldo* books is to find the hiding Waldo and in *Blue's Clues*, the typical function of the paw prints is to provide clues to the ultimate answer of a mystery. That is, the original intent of the story or character must be maintained and used in a parallel relationship to be effective.

Token System

Token systems allow the child to collect a predetermined number of tokens over a predetermined period of time in order to earn a predetermined reward. For example, the child is asked what he would like to "work for" or "earn" during a set amount of time or number of tasks. The choice is indicated on the token card along with the number of tokens needed to receive it. As the child accomplishes a task or demonstrates a desired behavior, he is given a token to place on his card. When all the required tokens are earned, the child is allowed to collect the reward that he chose.

Sample Token Card

Token	Token	Token

Working for ...

For additional information:

Hudson, J. (2006). *Prescription for success: Supporting children with autism spectrum disorders in the medical environment.* Shawnee Mission, KS: Autism Asperger Publishing Company.

5-Point Scale

The 5-point scale breaks down an abstract idea or concept, such as modulating proximity when engaging with others in conversation, into a clear, concrete, visual number system that can be more easily interpreted and modulated. The numbers range from 1 to 5 on each scale and may be modulated from the top down (5 to 1) or from the bottom up (1 to 5), depending on the goal of the scale and the representation of each number. Scales can be expanded to also indicate the reaction and response desired of the child and of the adults affected by the scale. When possible, the child should be the lead in defining each aspect of the scale. Sometimes a story is written to introduce the scale, giving a description of the problem and identifying the use of the scale for modulation.

Sample 5-Point Scale

Name: Colton		My Control	Scale
Rating	Looks like	Feels like	I can *try* to
5	Kicking or hitting	My head will probably explode	Call my mom go home
4	Screaming at people <u>Almost</u> hitting	Nervous	Go to see Mr. Peterson
3	Quiet sometimes rude talk	Bad mood grumpy	Stay away from kids (The ones I don't like!)
2	Regular kid – <u>not</u> weird!	Good	Enjoy it while it lasts
1	Playing hockey	A million bucks $	Stay that way!

From *The Incredible 5-Point Scale, (p. 29)*, by K. Buron & M. Curtis, 2003, Shawnee Mission, KS: Autism Asperger Publishing Company. Reprinted with permission.

For additional information:

Buron, K., & Curtis, M. (2003). *The incredible 5-point scale: Assisting students with autism spectrum disorders in understanding social interactions and controlling their emotions.* Shawnee Mission, KS: Autism Asperger Publishing Company.

Blank 5-Point Scale

Name: _____ My _____ Scale

Rating	Looks like	Feels like	I can *try* to
5			
4			
3			
2			
1			

From *The Incredible 5-Point Scale, (p. 71),* by K. Buron & M. Curtis, 2003, Shawnee Mission, KS: Autism Asperger Publishing Company. Reprinted with permission.

Transition Cue

Transition cues assist the child in moving through a series of activities or steps in an event. A cue is established by the child and created as a visual or concrete object. As each step is completed or accomplished, the child adjusts his transition cue to indicate that one fewer step is left. The cue may involve collecting an item or marking off a space on a card; the main thing is that it must indicate that transition is occurring and that time is decreasing.

Sample Transition Cue

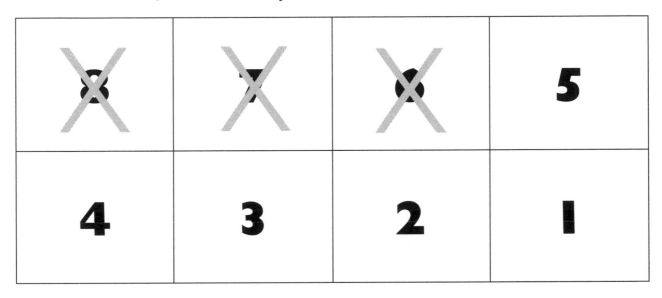

For additional information:

Hodgdon, L. (1995). *Visual strategies for improving communication: Practical supports for school and home.* Troy, MI: Quirk Roberts Publishing.

Blueprint

SUPPORT	STRATEGY	DESIRED OUTCOME
Waiting plan		
Communication		
Social		
Visual		
Hidden curriculum		
Sensory		
Motivation		
Behavior		

Hudson, J., & Bixler Coffin, A. (2007). *Out and About: Preparing Children with Autism Spectrum Disorders to Participate in Their Communities.* Shawnee Mission, KS: Autism Asperger Publishing Company (www.asperger.net). Used with permission.

Transition		
For sibling or other students		
Additional activities for school:		
Additional activities for home:		
REWIND		

Hudson, J., & Bixler Coffin, A. (2007). *Out and About: Preparing Children with Autism Spectrum Disorders to Participate in Their Communities.* Shawnee Mission, KS: Autism Asperger Publishing Company (www.asperger.net). Used with permission.

REFERENCES

Arwood, E. L., & Kaulitz, C. (2007). *Learning with a visual brain in an auditory world.* Shawnee Mission, KS: Autism Asperger Publishing Company.

Bellini, S. (2006). *Building social relationships: A systematic approach to teaching social interaction skills to children and adolescents with autism spectrum disorders and other social difficulties.* Shawnee Mission, KS: Autism Asperger Publishing Company.

Bieber, J. (Producer). (1994). *Learning disabilities and social skills with Richard Lavoie: Last one picked ... first one picked on.* Washington, DC: Public Broadcasting Service.

Bondy, A., & Frost, L. (2001). *A picture's worth: PECS and other visual communication strategies in autism.* Bethesda, MD: Woodbine House Publisher.

Bregman J. D., Zager, D., & Gerdtz, J. (2005) Behavioral interventions. In F. Volkmar, R. Paul, A. Klin, & D. Cohen (Eds.), *Handbook of autism and pervasive developmental disorders* (3rd ed., pp. 863-881). Hoboken, NJ: John Wiley & Sons, Inc.

Buron, K., & Curtis, M. (2003). *The incredible 5-point scale: Assisting students with autism spectrum disorders in understanding social interactions and controlling their emotions.* Shawnee Mission, KS: Autism Asperger Publishing Company.

Coucouvanis, J. (2005). *Super skills: A social skills group program for children with Asperger Syndrome, high-functioning autism and related challenges.* Shawnee Mission, KS: Autism Asperger Publishing Company.

Gagnon, E. (2001). *Power cards: Using special interests to motivate children and youth with Asperger Syndrome and autism.* Shawnee Mission, KS: Autism Asperger publishing Company.

Gray, C. (1994). *Comic strip conversations: Colorful, illustrated interactions with students with autism and related disorders.* Jenison, MI: Jenison Public Schools.

Gray, C. (1995). *Social Stories™ unlimited: Teaching social skills with social stories and comic strip conversations.* Jenison, MI: Jenison Public Schools.

Gray, C. (1998). *The advanced Social Story™ workbook.* Jenison, MI: Jenison Public Schools.

Hannah, L. (2001). *Teaching young children with autistic spectrum disorders to learn.* London: National Autism Society.

Hodgdon, L. (1995). *Visual strategies for improving communication: Practical supports for school and home.* Troy, MI: Quirk Roberts Publishing.

Hudson, J. (2006). *Prescription for success: Supporting children with autism spectrum disorders in the medical environment.* Shawnee Mission, KS: Autism Asperger Syndrome Publishing Company.

Mayo, P., & Waldo, P. (1986). *Scripting: Social communication for adolescents.* Eau Claire, WI: Thinking Publications.

McClannahan, L., & Krants, P. (2005). *Teaching conversation to children with autism: Scripts and script fading.* Bethesda, MD: Woodbine House Publisher.

Myles, B. S., & Adreon, D. (2001). *Asperger Syndrome and adolescence: Practical solutions for school success.* Shawnee Mission, KS: Autism Asperger Publishing Company.

Olley, J. G. (2005). Curriculum and classroom structure. In F. Volkmar, R. Paul, A. Klin, & D. Cohen (Eds.), *Handbook of autism and pervasive developmental disorders* (3rd ed., pp. 863-881). Hoboken, NJ: John Wiley & Sons, Inc.

Quill, K. (2000). DO-WATCH-LISTEN-SAY: *Social and communication intervention for children with autism.* Baltimore: Paul H. Brookes.

Savner, J. L., & Myles, B. S. (2000). *Making visual supports work in the home and community: Strategies for individuals with autism and Asperger Syndrome.* Shawnee Mission, KS: Autism Asperger Publishing Company.

Time Timer Inc. – www.timetimer.com

Wiig, E., & Wilson, C. (2001). *Map it out: Visual tools for thinking, organizing and communicating.* Eau Claire, WI: Thinking Publications.

Wilde, L. D., Koegel, L. K., & Koegel, R. L. (1992). *Increasing success in school through priming: A training manual.* Santa Barbara: University of California.

Other Books by Jill Hudson

Prescription for Success: Supporting Children with Autism Spectrum Disorders in the Medical Environment

Because of the unique needs of children with ASD, it is important to pay special attention to the details of their experience in the medical environment. Designed to help make the medical experience easier for all involved, this book presents information on ASD, the varying developmental levels, interventions, and assessments that medical staff, parents, educators, and key service providers can use to more effectively interact with and support children with ASD while in the medical setting. A CD at the back of the book includes forms and worksheets that can be printed and duplicated. ISBN 1931282951

Free CD includes forms, activities and games

Code 9966   **Price $24.95**

.

Cabins, Canoes, and Campfires: Guidelines for Establishing a Camp for Children with Autism Spectrum Disorders

Many children with autism spectrum disorders are not able to thrive in a typical summer camp due to their unique sensory and behavioral needs. Yet, like all other kids, most love the camp experience. To help make this dream become a reality, the author presents step-by-step how to put on a camp that takes into consideration the special needs of children on the autism spectrum. Based on her extensive personal experience both as a camper and a camp facilitator, Jill Hudson builds a camp from the ground up: from deciding on a mission and vision, advertising the camp, assessing the needs of each camper, to the physical camp layout, daily activities and more. Throughout the focus remains on the adjustments that need to be made to accommodate children on the autism spectrum during the camp experience. ISBN 1931282773

Code 9949   **Price: $19.95**

Autism Asperger Publishing Company
Visit www.asperger.net or call 877.277.8254 to place an order.

AAPC Exclusive

The best-selling practical solutions series continues to offer sound, practical advice for and about individuals with ASD and other social-cognitive disorders. These titles offer a range of topics – from sensory issues to social situations and education to behavior – that address the needs of individuals on the spectrum. These books truly offer "practical solutions" to everyday challenges people with ASD face.

Asperger Syndrome and Difficult Moments: Practical Solutions for Tantrums, Rage, and Meltdowns (Revised and Expanded Edition)

Brenda Smith Myles and Jack Southwick

Code 9901B   Price: $21.95
Code 9720 (DVD)   Price: $29.95

Asperger Syndrome and Adolescence: Practical Solutions for School Success

Brenda Smith Myles, Ph.D., and Diane Adreon

Code 9908   Price: $23.95

Asperger Syndrome and Sensory Issues: Practical Solutions for Making Sense of the World

Brenda Smith Myles, Katherine Tapscott Cook, Nancy E. Miller, Louann Rinner, and Lisa A. Robbins

Code 9907A   Price: $21.95

Asperger Syndrome and the Elementary School Experience: Practical Solutions for Academic & Social Difficulties

Susan Thompson Moore

Code 9911   Price: $23.95

Autism Asperger Publishing Company

Practical Solutions Series

Practical Solutions to Everyday Challenges for Children with Asperger Syndrome

Haley Morgan Myles

Code 9917   **Price: $13.95**

The Hidden Curriculum: Practical Solutions for Understanding Unstated Rules in Social Situations

Brenda Smith Myles, Melissa L. Trautman, and Ronda L. Schelvan

Code 9942 (book)   **Price: $19.95**
Code 9721 (DVD)   **Price: $29.95**
Code 9968 (calendar)   **see website for price**

Perfect Targets: Asperger Syndrome and Bullying; Practical Solutions for Surviving the Social World

Rebekah Heinrichs

Code 9918   **Price: $21.95**

Finding Our Way: Practical Solutions for Creating a Supportive Home and Community for the Asperger Syndrome Family

Kristi Sakai

Code 9948   **Price: $21.95**

Visit www.asperger.net or call 877.277.8254 to place an order.

A PC

Autism Asperger Publishing Co.
P.O. Box 23173
Shawnee Mission, Kansas 66283-0173
www.asperger.net